CHANGE OUR HEARTS
Daily Meditations for Lent

RORY COONEY

Franciscan
MEDIA
Cincinnati, Ohio

Excerpts are taken from "Change Our Hearts," by Rory Cooney. ©1984, Spirit & Song, a division of OCP, 5536 NE Hassalo, Portland, OR 97213. All rights reserved. Used with permission. Scripture passages have been taken from *New Revised Standard Version Bible,* copyright ©1989 by the Division of Christian Education of the National Council of the Churches of Christ in the U.S.A., and used by permission. All rights reserved.

Cover design by Sean Foster
Cover image © Fotolia | Vilnis
Book design by Mark Sullivan

LIBRARY OF CONGRESS CATALOGING-IN-PUBLICATION DATA
Cooney, Rory, 1952-
Change our hearts : daily meditations for Lent / Rory Cooney.
    pages cm
Includes bibliographical references and index.
ISBN 978-1-61636-725-1 (alk. paper)
1. Lent—Prayers and devotions. 2. Common lectionary (1992) I. Title.
BX2170.L4.C63 2013
242'.34—dc23
                            2013037601

ISBN 978-1-61636-725-1

Published by Franciscan Media
28 W. Liberty St.
Cincinnati, OH 45202
www.FranciscanMedia.org

Printed in the United States of America.
Printed on acid-free paper.
14 15 16 17 18   5 4 3 2 1

INTRODUCTION

"In the liturgy and the liturgical catechesis of Lent the reminder of baptism already received or the preparation for its reception, as well as the theme of repentance, renew the entire community along with those being prepared to celebrate the paschal mystery, in which each of the elect will share through the sacraments of initiation. For both the elect and the local community, therefore, the Lenten season is a time for spiritual recollection in preparation for the celebration of the Paschal mystery."[1]

The lectionary readings chosen for Lent each year are like a crash course in Christianity, a road map for the journey to Easter. For those who are to be initiated at the Easter Vigil, they offer a summons to the fullness of Christian life into which they have been apprenticed for months or years. For those who are baptized, their images and words echo and resonate with a call to deeper conversion, and throw light onto the insidious ways that the world of the gods other than the Abba of Jesus have seduced and narcotized us into habits of sin. At the same time, they stir in all of us a desire to live up to the blessed calling that we have received, and to use our many gifts for building up the reign of God.

As we prepare to renew our baptismal promises to reject sin and live the Gospel this Easter, I invite you to follow this lectionary path with me, the freedom highway that passes through both the desert and the middle of the sea.

> Brought by your hand to the edge of our
>   dreams,
> One foot in paradise, one in the waste,
> Drawn by your promises, still, we are lured
> By the shadows and the chains we leave
>   behind, but
> Change our hearts this time:
> Your word says it can be.
> Change our minds this time:
> Your life could make us free.
> We are the people your call set apart
> Lord, this time change our hearts.

ASH WEDNESDAY
JOEL 2:12–18; PSALMS 51:3–4, 5–6, 12–13, 14,17; 2
CORINTHIANS 5:20—6:2; MATTHEW 6:1–6, 16–18

We don't know what precipitated the prophet Joel's call to the national fast in today's First Reading. Whatever it was, a plague of locusts or foreign invaders, there is urgency to the call. Everyone, even new mothers and newlyweds, needs to turn mind and heart to God and begin a national fasting. God is upset with us now, and it is now that we need to turn back to him.

We ourselves may have a more nuanced theology of catastrophe. Jesus rejected the idea that calamity was the result of personal sin. What we perceive as blessing or curse is not necessarily God's doing. But there are consequences of human actions. We are connected to each other in ways we don't even perceive. The good that we do, the ways that we act selflessly and thoughtfully for others change the world for the better. Our acts of greed and violence, on the other hand, also have consequences in the world that rebound on us as well. Eventually, we all drink from the well that we have poisoned.

Baptism and the baptismal promises are the outward sign of a radical choice into which we grow as infants or into which we are formed as adults. Baptism into Christ forms us in the way of the cross, the way of unconditional love, *agape*, that is at the heart of the paschal mystery. We come to know that we are responsible for one another, especially the poor and powerless, because God's own heart is with them.

We think we have more time, but the word of God says that the time for a change is now. "The reign of God is at hand. Turn away from sin, and believe the good news." Ash Wednesday reminds us that our actions have consequences. The time for choosing the Gospel is now. This is the day of salvation.

PRACTICE: Receive and feel the cross of ashes today. Hear the words, "Turn away from sin, and believe." Remember that we are dust (Genesis 3:19); reread Genesis 2:6–7, and remember what God does with dust, a little water, and divine breath.

THURSDAY AFTER ASH WEDNESDAY
DEUTERONOMY 30:15–20; PSALMS 1:1–2, 3–4, 6; LUKE 9:22–25

Take up your cross, and follow me.

As they are made catechumens, adults are signed from head to toe and all over with the cross. They are thus "branded" as Christians. Even in the rite of infant baptism, the priest, parents, and godparents sign the baby's forehead with a cross.

This is a solemn, sobering moment. The cross, for Jesus and his contemporaries, was not a symbol of anything. It was an instrument of torture and terror reserved for the enemies of Caesar. The cross as a symbol of God or life would have been repulsive to anyone who lived in the Roman Empire. Hundreds, sometimes thousands, were crucified at a time during periods of insurrection, their bodies left on the crosses as a warning to others who would disturb the *Pax Romana*.

The resurrection of Jesus, and time, changed all of that. Yes, the journey to the cross is also the disciple's journey. But today we hear it with the words of Deuteronomy echoing in the background, that our choice is between life and death. Choosing the cross, then, is choosing life. But how can that be?

The cross is the sign of the choice we make that life in the *Pax Romana*, or the *Pax Americana*, or any other peace as the world gives it is not enough for us. Caesar, in every time and every country, only brings violence, death, and fear into the world. Peace that isn't for everyone isn't peace at all. Jesus offers another God to us, the God of justice, peace, and love, and asks us to believe in that God, his Abba, our Father.

Our baptismal promises call us to reject false gods and sin, and believe in God, Jesus, Spirit, and Church. We have forty days to identify the ways we've compromised with death in order to get along in Caesar's world, and to ask for divine light to guide our choices for life going forward.

PRACTICE: Use Lent to reconnect with the sign of the cross, especially when using baptismal water as you enter the church. Remember that the fidelity of

Jesus led him to the cross. Today he invites us again to join his journey.

FRIDAY AFTER ASH WEDNESDAY
ISAIAH 58:1–9A; PSALMS 51:3–4, 5–6AB, 18–19; MATTHEW 9:14–15

Twice already, three days into Lent, we've heard about fasting as a discipline. What is fasting for Christians?

There is a thread that goes throughout the season of Lent, from Ash Wednesday through the Fourth Sunday and up through the renewal of baptismal promises, that religion has to be constantly monitored for integrity, and reformed so that it honors the right God, the Abba of Jesus. The exhortations to prayer, almsgiving, and fasting that we heard Wednesday from the Sermon on the Mount were not exhortations to heroic levels of the practices, but warnings that all religious practices should originate from the heart and be performed out of love, and not to make others think we are pious. Twice in the Lenten Gospels Jesus heals on the Sabbath, breaking religious law. He forces the question about who God is and what God wants. Does God want religion or does God want merciful love?

The prophets answer this question for us as a corrective to priestly and royal strains that also run through Scripture. Possibly no prophet answers more clearly than Isaiah in today's First Reading. This is the fasting that God seeks: Not just occasional ritual fasting, but freedom for captives, bread for the hungry, housing for the homeless, clothing for the naked, solidarity with all.

Physical fasting is sacramental. It shows a desire to choose the other, a setting aside of personal comfort and even health for as a gesture of love and solidarity. It carries with it an inkling that good news for the poor will require the emptying of self, paying a cost out of our own livelihood as an act of loving reparation, in order to preach that good news authentically. Doing God's will, fasting or otherwise, is focused on other people, not on personal fulfillment. *Kenosis,* pouring out of the self, is oriented toward giving life to others, not suicide. Fasting is God-like to the extent that it shares in *agape*.

PRAYER: Take my hunger today, Jesus, and fill me with the Gospel. May my hunger, and the gift of my goods, fill my neighbor's belly, so that my neighbor may know that you are a God who wants their needs met more than you desire my noisy prayers. Amen.

SATURDAY AFTER ASH WEDNESDAY
ISAIAH 58:9B–14; PSALMS 86:1–2, 3–4, 5–6; LUKE 5:27–32

Compromise can be seen either as a virtue or a vice. On the one hand, a politician can be lauded as a "great compromiser" when he is able to bring two opposing sides of an argument out from a place of stasis and recrimination to a new place of agreement and progress. On the other hand, being accused of compromising the core values of a group might lead to being marginalized or even ostracized in times of deep political entrenchment.

Collaborators in a time of occupation, people who are employed by or cooperate with the occupiers, rarely fare well. Stories of the treatment of collaborators in modern wars are as terrifying as they are illustrative of the tension between instincts for survival and solidarity.

Enter Levi and the tax collectors, collaborators with the occupying Romans. They were Jews who served Caesar, the god of Rome. As such, they were despised by the populace and regarded as sinners by the Temple elite. Jesus, however, takes a different approach with Levi, saying: "Follow me." Dinner ensues, along with the predictable polemics with the orthodox.

It's clear that both Levi and Jesus know that "follow me" means "turn your back on what you're doing." Jesus is not following Caesar, and he is not fooled by the collaborating religiosity of the Temple. Levi can't be happy with his chosen way of life. He sees in Jesus what he might yet become: the faithful Jew that God might make of him. Like the psalmist sings today, he sings, "Teach me your ways."

"Follow me" still means turning our back on the other god-emperors who claim our allegiance, and require our collaboration. What is required of us is leaving everything. We know in our hearts we have everything to gain. Can we move, this year, together, toward the empire of God? Can it be our voice that calls the unfulfilled collaborator to a new life with the simple words, "Follow me"?

PRAYER: Teach me your ways, O Lord. Help me to turn away from the empty promises of greed and death, and show me the gifts within me that will repair the breaches between us, and move your people toward your reign of justice and peace. Amen.

───── ❦ ─────

FIRST SUNDAY OF LENT
YEAR A: GENESIS 2:7–9; 3:1–7; PSALMS 51:3–4, 5–6, 12–13, 17; ROMANS 5:12–19; MATTHEW 4:1–11

YEAR B: GENESIS 9:8–15; PSALMS 25:4–5, 6–7, 8–9; 1 PETER 3:18–22; MARK 1:12–15

YEAR C: DEUTERONOMY 26:4–10; PSALMS 91:1–2, 10–11, 12–13, 14–15; ROMANS 10:8–13; LUKE 4:1–13

In cathedral churches all over the world today, bishops will make the astounding declaration that people we ourselves know, people with whom we have prayed, worked, served, and laughed, have been chosen by God for the Easter sacraments. What a statement! Because of the testimony of their lives, of their godparents, catechists, clergy, and all of us, the bishop says that God has chosen them to be initiated into the Church, chosen them to be part of Christ. This rite, called the Rite of Election because the catechumens are elected (i.e., chosen) for initiation, is associated with the First Sunday of Lent.

In the book of Genesis, God hand-made, literally, Adam and Eve to be his own. He walked with them in the cool of the garden. But as the story unfolds, being human wasn't enough for them. The tempter told Eve, "Your eyes will be opened, and you will be like gods." It's better to be a god. Being a human being, Satan implies, is for losers. In Genesis, Adam and Eve go their own way, and it leads out of the garden, out of paradise.

But Jesus, fresh out of the Jordan's water and with "You are my beloved" still ringing in his ears, doesn't fall for that. Now the tempter tries to get Jesus to realize that to be human is to be a loser. "Something special about you, boy," he seems to say. "Turn these stones to bread, feed yourself and everybody else. God will rescue you from death. Follow me." But Jesus knows the difference between love and empty promises and chooses to obey his calling, and pursue the course of being God's anointed wherever it may lead.

Decisions matter. God has made a choice for us. Now, we are invited to choose. On Easter, will we choose empty promises or the empire of love? For us, it's just a matter of turning around, and taking that first step into the desert.

PRACTICE: Be the voice of God, and call someone "beloved." Let them know that their gifts matter, and that they are "called for the victory of justice."

MONDAY OF THE FIRST WEEK OF LENT
LEVITICUS 19:1–2, 11–18; PSALMS 19:8, 9, 10, 15;
MATTHEW 25:31–46

Matthew 25 is the story of Christianity's final exam. Notice what's missing from the syllabus. No questions about God. No questions about the sacraments. No questions about whom we married or where we went to church. The teacher, or in this parable, the king, says to one group: "Come unto me, blessed of my Father, into the kingdom prepared for you since the foundation of the world. I needed you in the real world, the world of hunger, thirst, loneliness, and cold, and you were there with food, water, friendship, and clothing." To others, the king says, "Depart from me, out of my sight. I needed you in the real world, the world of hunger, thirst, loneliness, and cold, and you pretended you didn't see me."

And everybody is confused. "What is he talking about? When did we see you? When did we ignore you?" You know the punch line. "Whenever you did it for anyone, however small or insignificant, you did it for me."

The First Reading from Leviticus is about the way that the Israelites ought to treat one another, that is, other Israelites. But lest we think that the borders of the family, town, or nation limn the boundaries of the law, the same chapter, a few verses later, makes explicit the commandment to "love the alien as yourself."

Today's liturgy points us to our destination and shepherds us toward new behaviors. "Get real," the Word of God seems to be saying. "Don't let your pious thoughts delude you into thinking that you have a ticket to heaven." In the incarnation, God pitched a tent with the human race because we needed him, and so service of God begins and ends with being with others and serving their needs. That is the master's way, and no servant is greater than the master.

Until about the sixth century, this was the first day of Lent. And what a lesson we have on day one! We love and serve the other because that's what

God does. That is the Word of God, the word of spirit and life.

PRACTICE: Use Matthew 25:31–45 as a beginning-of-Lent inventory on your commitment to living the Gospel. Make it an examination of conscience. Get real.

TUESDAY OF THE FIRST WEEK OF LENT
ISAIAH 55:10–11; PSALMS 34:4–5, 6–7, 16–17, 18–19; MATTHEW 6:7–15

Newly elect or cradle Catholic, we still employ the three traditional disciplines of Lent as we prepare to renew our baptismal promises on Easter: fasting, almsgiving, and prayer. We may have neglected these Christian habits as paths to union with God and one another, but Lent calls us back to them, and teaches us their wisdom again.

Today's Scriptures are, at first glance, specifically concerned with prayer. The centerpiece of the Gospel is Matthew's version of the Lord's Prayer. But as you sit with the readings today, hear the entire Gospel in the light of the reading from Isaiah and the psalm, and perhaps another aspect will emerge.

What I hear is that we consider a different God from the one we think we know, the one we are sometimes told we ought to believe in. This God already knows what we need before we ask for it, and furthermore, according to Psalm 34, wants to rescue us from distress, and be joy and comfort to the brokenhearted. God's Word, God's self-expression in Christ, will accomplish God's will in the world. This God does not want to be known as emperor or judge or bookkeeper, but as Father. And not just as a Father, but as Our Father. We pray to God communally, or at least with a clear awareness that in naming God we are claimed by one another as family, and our relationship to one another defines our relationship to him.

Twice in today's Gospel forgiveness of debt is mentioned. We may not know the purpose of prayer, or whether our prayers somehow change God. But we can be sure that if we practice forgiveness as we are reminded every time we pray the Lord's Prayer,

prayer will change us. Then our image of God might change, and seeing God as Jesus did, generous, forgiving, bowing down, a Father, we might finally begin to forgive ourselves and have compassion for one another.

PRACTICE: If you wish, pray today for one of the elect in your parish, or for all the elect in your diocese. Or be the jubilee of God, and forgive someone a debt. Take a little turn toward "thy kingdom come."

WEDNESDAY OF THE FIRST WEEK OF LENT
JONAH 3:1–10; PSALMS 51:3–4, 12–13, 18–19; LUKE 11:29–32

As a reading in the liturgy, the Jonah story today is held in its orbit by the Gospel and the Responsorial Psalm, so that the light and energy of each reflects on the other. Hear in the background the words of the baptismal promises, like those eight notes grounding Pachelbel's *Canon*, above which sparkle all of those Baroque embellishments, airy and interdependent.

Jonah is a prophet gone off the rails, a prophet so sure of what God ought to do that he doesn't leave room for God to do it. In the end he is successful but shipwrecked, unhappy, and a laughingstock. Jonah is sent to preach repentance in Nineveh, the capital of pagan Assyria. He tries to escape his mission by sea, but is thrown overboard, swallowed by a big fish, and vomited onto the shore of Assyria. Defeated, he fulfills his mission and preaches repentance to the pagans. All of them, including the king, repent. How does Jonah react? He gets angry. He was looking forward to the fire and brimstone.

In the Gospel, Jesus speaks of the sign of Jonah and the "queen of the south." Both of these stories represent people from outside the tradition coming to know the God whom the tradition reveals, sometimes with greater faith than the keepers of the tradition themselves. We insiders attempt to measure God's mercy out with teaspoons, when all the time it's pouring over us like a river.

The signs of God-among-us are not limited to the people we know in our church, those who are just like us. Wherever we can discern that healing is taking place, where breaches between people are mended, where people are giving their lives so that other people might live fuller, better lives, that is where God is. To believe in God is to believe in surprising grace, and to believe that healing, hope, and community are already present in the world. Mostly, to believe in God requires that we give up on the idea that we are God, passing judgment on the motives and morality of others. That alone is a good project for any Lent.

PRAYER: My eyes are on you alone, O God. Let me see you in all I do, in all whom I meet, and in all that I desire. Amen.

THURSDAY OF THE FIRST WEEK OF LENT
ESTHER C:12, 14–16, 23–25; PSALMS 138:1–2AB, 2CDE–3, 7C–8; MATTHEW 7:7–12

Why do we pray intercessory prayer, asking God to do things we think we want or need? Is it possible that Christians praying together, if we could even settle on something to pray for in the same way, could somehow change God's mind? And if it's hard to imagine that about all Christians praying for a thing together, what about when I'm praying about my job, or my boss, or my marriage, or my children? Couldn't I just save a lot of time by just praying, "God, I'm going to do the best I can, but please handle the details. I'll try to understand it later."

Two thoughts here. First, if I'm honest, I have to say that sometimes prayer does seem to "work," whatever that means. Either a situation changes or I change or both, but in some way my whole person is satisfied that somehow prayer made a difference in my life.

Second, when I try to discern the why of prayer, it comes down to one of those answers from early in childhood. Does this conversation sound familiar to you?

Me: But Mom, why? Why do I have to read/do/clean that?

Mom: Because I told you to.

I guess that it has to be all right, sometimes, not to understand the why of the spiritual life, and just submit to it because we are told to. Holy people who have lived life before us and left signs along the pathway for us assure us that prayer is not wasted time, whether it works or not. We pray intercessory prayer in the liturgy itself, which is to say that it's part of the very fabric of what the Church does when we're most ourselves.

The situation of Queen Esther, using her charm and wit to defend her people against the hatred and genocidal whim of Xerxes, relied on prayer so that God might notice her people's plight, remember their relationship, and intervene. I suppose the peasants gathered for the Sermon on the Mount did not live in the best of times or places either. Maybe there's something to the Golden Rule that Jesus doesn't tell us: Maybe God lives by it too?

PRACTICE: What is most on your mind right now? For what do you need to pray? Spend some time today asking God to help you with this, and be open to how your prayer is answered.

FRIDAY OF THE FIRST WEEK OF LENT
EZEKIEL 18:21–28; PSALMS 130:1–2, 3–4, 5–7A, 7BC–8;
MATTHEW 5:20–26

Once we accept the premise that, in the community of Christ, God is Father, or head of the household, then the first correlative is that we are all related to one another as brothers and sisters. The Gospel does not imagine that this is just a nice idea or a metaphor. There are implications for the community as there were for Jesus that resulted from his understanding of God as Father of all.

In fact, "life with Father" means that everyone has to step up from the law, with its "thou shalt nots" and prescriptions and proscriptions, into the realm of love. This love is not love that feels like being good because it makes us feel good, nor is it motivated only by bonds of honor or family affection. The Christian is called to imitate God who is *agape*, creating, healing, other-centered, unconditional love. *Agape* knows that sharing life does not diminish it. Rather, life springs, inexhaustible, from the very nature of God. Love is not divided. It multiplies.

Today we hear that it's not enough to refrain from killing when have a disagreement with a neighbor. We have to live as though our survival as a community depends on every relationship. It's easy, Jesus implies, to have the kind of bean-counting righteousness that avoids murder but feels entitled to harbor loathing in the heart, or fire the poison-tipped arrows of the tongue toward another.

Abba doesn't want praise from those who act like that. On your way to church with resentment in your heart? Forget about church. Go and make peace with the other person. Why? Because that's how Abba wants it. That's how Abba does it, in fact. This is a God who doesn't revel in sacrifice and glut on praise, but one who wants an empire where peace on earth is the glory in heaven.

It's never too late to make the change, either. Hard-hearted as we may be, however many years it takes for divine *agape* to soften our hearts and waken them to grace, God is already waiting with forgiveness, kindness, and plenteous redemption.

No one said it was going to be easy. But family life never is.

PRAYER: Lord, break this heart of stone and let me live in your love forever. Help me be a person of peace, one who reconciles without thought of my own gain. Amen.

SATURDAY OF THE FIRST WEEK OF LENT
DEUTERONOMY 26:16–19; PSALMS 119:1–2, 4–5, 7–8;
MATTHEW 5:43–48

One of the lines from the Sermon on the Mount that haunts me, and ought to haunt all of us who were born into the Church and feel any sense of entitlement or satisfaction in our parishes, are those cajoling words from today's Gospel, one of the most under-preached and over-spiritualized in all of Christendom.

> For if you love those who love you, what reward do you have? Do not even the tax collectors do the same? And if you greet your

brothers and sisters only, what more are you doing than others? Do not even the Gentiles do the same?

It's worth asking ourselves about every Lenten project we undertake, every parish endeavor, everything we do in the Christian life. Do not the Gentiles do the same? What makes us different? How will anyone know that we follow Christ and not just the altruistic best of our nature? I'm not suggesting, nor was Jesus, that altruism is bad, or that loving those who love us is bad. In fact, that is what is expected. But from those who are baptized into the paschal God, who have been called into Christ to spread the good news of reconciliation to the whole world, it's not enough.

The call to *agape* extends beyond the boundaries of the baptized and even beyond the boundaries of sympathizers and people of good will. We are to love our enemies, and do good to those who hate us. Why? Because God does it, and we are summoned to be perfect as God is perfect.

Renewing our baptismal promise to reject sin, that is, the way of the false gods, means that we need to reject hatred, prejudice, violence, retribution, vengeance, and war. Renewing our baptism promise to believe in (that is, give our love to) God means that we need to embrace the good of the enemy and the hater with the same desire for their good in this world as we do any brother or sister or friend in the household of the faithful.

It really is as simple, and as staggeringly difficult, as that. Already, at the end of this first full week of Lent, the cross looms nearer than we had first imagined.

PRACTICE: Whom do you consider your brother and your sister? Who is not? Take a look at the reasons you exclude some people from the gaze of love we are called to cast on everyone. How would God react to your excuses?

SECOND SUNDAY OF LENT

YEAR A: GENESIS 12:1–4A; PSALMS 33:4–5, 18–19, 20, 22; 2 TIMOTHY 1:8–10; MATTHEW 17:1–9

YEAR B: GENESIS 22:1–2, 9A, 10–13, 15–18; PSALMS 116:10, 15, 16–17, 18–19; ROMANS 8:31B–34; MARK 9:2–10

YEAR C: GENESIS 15:5–12, 17–18; PSALMS 27:1, 7–8A, 8B–9, 13–14; PHILIPPIANS 3:17—4:1; LUKE 9:28B–36

The words spoken in Genesis to Abram are spoken to all of us who want to follow Christ, who want to turn away from sin and believe the good news. "Go from your country…to the land that I will show you." Consider that: Leave what you know, take everyone along, and trust me to lead you somewhere better. These may sound like simple tasks. But they are immense journeys once undertaken, difficult, and full of danger.

The Second Letter to Timothy speaks with the voice of St. Paul in his last days, facing an imminent time of departure and preparing for that *transitus*. He exhorts the reader, "Join with me in suffering for the Gospel, relying on the power of God." The cross, or for St. Paul, the sword, looms.

Eyes fixed on the Jerusalem road, Jesus is transfigured on the mountain, and seen speaking with Moses and Elijah. Why them? Moses and Elijah also found themselves in dire straits as men who spoke for God. They were the subjects of intense manhunts and persecution by rulers and, in Elijah's case, religious leaders as well. Jesus was about to enter their number. Surely he had calculated the career trajectory of preaching of a God other than Caesar.

The Transfiguration represents a moment when he could once again bask in the overwhelming sense of being possessed by divine favor. "This is my beloved." The voice that spoke over the Jordan at his baptism offers him hope and courage to face the Jerusalem road.

Can we be that for one another? Can our community be a place where we find affirmation, creative strategy, and hope amid the confrontations that will inevitably ensue in our peaceful quest for justice, peace, and equality in this world? Let us be a voice that calls each one "beloved" brother or sister. Let us be companions on the journey to the cross and encourage one another in hope for what might lie beyond.

PRACTICE: Let nothing negative about another person escape your mouth today. When you're tempted, identify what it is about yourself that you want to lash out about, and pray for healing for both of you.

MONDAY OF THE SECOND WEEK OF LENT
DANIEL 9:4B–10; PSALMS 79:8, 9, 11, 13; LUKE 6:36–38

Today's Gospel picks up with the verse in Luke's "Sermon on the Plain" (6:36) that is the parallel to the last verse we heard on Saturday (Matthew 5:48). Here, Luke says, "Be merciful, just as your Father is merciful." Imitating the perfect mercy of God, who is "kind to the ungrateful and the wicked," is the point of both evangelists.

To say with integrity that I believe in God and in Christ, that I believe in the Holy Spirit and the Church and so on, is not merely to assent to a set of principles. Our word *belief* evolved from the same root as our word *love*. When the Jewish Shema was first articulated, that we should love the Lord our God with our whole heart, soul, mind, and strength, it was a way of saying "in every way that makes us people in this world." *Strength* didn't mean muscle power. It meant something like "muchness." Translated more directly, it means "with your wealth." Money. You know, where the first-world rubber hits the road.

The Jesuit priest and activist Daniel Berrigan famously remarked, "Your faith is rarely where your head is at. Or your heart. Your faith is where your ass is at! Where are you sitting? What are you involved in? Are you faithful to anything? That will show, or not show, the quality of your faith."[2] To believe in this God, the God of Jesus, the God to whom we are taught to pray as "Our Father," is to believe in a generous mercy that is bestowed not only upon the deserving, but upon the good and bad alike.

Furthermore, to believe in this God is to choose to imitate Christ, his Son, and to show the same unrestricted kindness. Our love should pour out unreservedly as presence, forgiveness, support, and healing. "Give and it will be given to you. A good measure, pressed down, shaken together, running over...."

Every journey of a thousand miles begins with a single step. And, as my mentor Fr. James Dunning used to say, "Anything worth doing is worth doing badly." It starts with conversion (turning around), and stepping in a new direction.

PRACTICE: What do you find worth doing today?

TUESDAY OF THE SECOND WEEK OF LENT
ISAIAH 1:10, 16–20; PSALMS 50:8–9, 16BC–17, 21, 23; MATTHEW 23:1–12

By the time of Jesus, the Temple leadership was in business with the Romans, both to procure its own survival as well as the survival and well-being of the populace. But survival is not life. Once the vision of the liberating God of Exodus has been compromised, it is a short journey to meaningless ritual. The religious establishment then models itself upon the rival god—in this case, Caesar, who accomplishes his will and vision by violence and shows of power.

In today's Gospel, Jesus, like the psalmist and Isaiah before him, takes the temple leaders to task for pretending to do holy work while in fact taking advantage of their fellow Israelites already debilitated by the hardships of peasant life in an occupied outpost of the empire. Jesus satirizes the Temple elite by calling them "actors," which is the kinder, more literal meaning of the Greek word translated as "hypocrites."

If we find ourselves trying to climb up the Church hierarchy, gain status through ministry, or do what we do for any reason other than the betterment of others' lives, we need to take a step back and discern which God we are serving. The arc of the God of Jesus is downward and outward; it seeks to give away, to ennoble, to share meaning. The paschal mystery reminds us Jesus revealed that kind of God to us; we have been baptized into that mystery, and not the grasping, controlling way of other gods. "All who exalt themselves will be humbled, and all who humble themselves will be exalted. The greatest among you will be your servant."

The apostles missed this pretty much right up to the Ascension. I don't blame them. It's not the way of the world, and that is the way we all know. But we've had two thousand years to assimilate the message. It should be different for us. Two thousand years, now forty days more, to learn to bow.

PRACTICE: Let's focus on integrity, knowing that our service at the altar is a sacrament of service: our service of the world, and God's service of us by sustaining us in fully human life.

WEDNESDAY OF THE SECOND WEEK OF LENT
JEREMIAH 18:18–20; PSALMS 31:5–6, 14, 15–16;
MATTHEW 20:17–28

Chesterton famously quipped that "Christianity has not been tried and found wanting; it has been found difficult and not tried."[3] There are a lot of religious leaders who will tell us whatever we want to hear. No one, it seems, has ever had trouble gathering people and founding a church. Widely followed spiritualities, inside and outside mainstream churches, promise material success and spiritual crosses, the opposite of the Gospel.

Jerusalem had priests and prophets in the days of Jeremiah (and Ezekiel, and others) who were perfectly willing to maintain the status quo, endorse the king, and keep their jobs. Accommodating forces within the Temple priesthood had forged an uneasy symbiosis with Rome through the Herodian puppet kings who were nominally Jewish. Jesus offered a choice to the oppressed population by asking them to return to the God of their covenant. Parodying the Temple priesthood and the rich in his parables, he offered those who hear him an alternative by contrasting the reign of God with their lives in the present. "How's that *Pax Romana* working out for you? Listen to what Abba has in store for you."

Jesus must have realized that his preaching would be seen both as blasphemous to the Temple leaders and to the occupying defenders of Roman civil religion. Crucifixion was reserved for enemies of Caesar, and he wanted his followers to understand that the cross, not just "hard times" or "spiritual difficulties" but wooden beams to which people were nailed with real nails, was a possible outcome of following him. But he did not change his message to accommodate fear, because he trusted in God to keep his side of the bargain.

"Are you getting all this?" he seems to be saying to the sons of Zebedee, their mother, and the other disciples. "This isn't about making a kingdom like Caesar's. It's about being like Abba. You achieve greatness by serving one another, because Abba is like that." That is the Christianity that has not been tried, not widely, at least. But it is the only true Christianity, the Christianity that actually has Christ in it.

PRACTICE: Whatever your sword is, put it away today. Let us lead by our example, and let our example be service.

THURSDAY OF THE SECOND WEEK OF LENT
JEREMIAH 17:5–10; PSALMS 1:1–2, 3, 4, 6; LUKE 16:19–31

Luke, more than the other evangelists, is explicit about the relationship between rich and poor in the reign of God. The parable of Lazarus and the Rich Man dramatizes the blindness that prevents us from seeing human need right before our eyes. What we believe, what we hope, and whom we trust shape our experience of the world. It's why the prophet Jeremiah claims that those who trust in human beings rather than God are cursed. Their hope is destined for disappointment or worse.

The Rich Man in the Gospel trusts in what he has to get him through the day. His wealth blinds him to the need of a poor man sitting right by his gate. In this parable, even the dogs are more attentive to Lazarus than the rich man. Luke isn't pulling any punches.

Don't all of us who are reading this today need to confess that in every sense we can conceive of, we are the rich man in this story? Aren't the poor right at our gates, so that we have to walk by them when we leave our homes or workplaces every day? What does this have to do with our renewal of baptismal promises?

To believe in God the Father, and in Jesus, and in the Holy Spirit, is to say that we don't believe in any other god, including gods of money, sex, and power. To believe is to act out of love, to change one's behavior. That is our Lenten struggle, to be people of integrity, to have our actions match our thoughts, and to have our thoughts match reality.

Who or what is it that we really worship? How can we tell whether we've moved toward the more just reign of God Jesus proposed as an alternative to the way we're living now? Well, in fact, someone has risen from the dead. We say that we believe that. Do we notice the poor sitting outside the doors of our homes, offices, and churches? Are they still poor?

PRACTICE: Set up a personal donation of time or money to help the poor, one designed to last beyond Lent. Solicit the charity of friends, too. That's what friends are for.

Friday of the Second Week of Lent
Genesis 37:3–4, 12–13a, 17b–28a; Psalms 105:16–17, 18–19, 20–21; Matthew 21:33–43, 45–46

Lent, as preparation for baptism, is preparation for dying of the old self and putting on the new person. With baptism, we can say, "It is no longer I who live, but it is Christ who lives in me" (Galatians 2:20). Paul reminds us in Romans that "you who were baptized into Christ Jesus were baptized into his death." The advent of the reign of God spells the end of all counterfeit gods, but they will not go easily. They will fight back with the fiercest weapons that they have at their disposal: fear and death.

It is important for us all to go into Christian life with our eyes open. This is not going to be a parade with flashing swords and guns and prisoners. The victory of the Father of Jesus will look like…what? Maybe a family picnic, with the stronger ones seeing to the needs of the weak, and the Father looking to be the greatest servant of all. Everyone is invited, and invited over and over again, with love and compassion. No threats or coercion will be allowed.

The story of Joseph and his brothers and the parable of the absentee landlord let us know that the chosen of God can expect violent resistance from those who want more. But both stories also contain stories of imminent, certain rescue. Joseph, the insignificant but beloved son of Jacob, by grace rises to the level of Pharaoh's chancellor. He could wreak vengeance on his brothers for their treachery. Instead, he plays a trick on them to waken them to their misdeeds and then shares his wealth to restore them. In the Gospel allegory of the vineyard, the restoration of the landlord's son is suggested by Jesus's use of Psalm 118 which every Christian associates with the Easter liturgy: "The stone that the builders rejected has become the chief cornerstone."

The liturgies of Triduum celebrate this dynamic. They show us how to deal with rejection and misunderstanding: Eat together, serve one another, put away your sword, give your life away and get it back better than before, indestructible. No vengeance toward the resisters, just mercy, forgiveness, and empowerment for change. Some who resisted became apostles. "Remember the marvels the Lord has done." God could do the same with us.

PRACTICE: Who is waiting for you to serve him or her? It could be someone in your family, or a friend or neighbor. Maybe there is a group that needs your assistance now. Consider this, and act on it.

SATURDAY OF THE SECOND WEEK OF LENT
MICAH 7:14–15, 18–20; PSALMS 103:1–2, 3–4, 9–10,
11–12; LUKE 15:1–3, 11–32

Luke 15 begins with a dig that comes from the opponents of Jesus's open table, "This fellow welcomes sinners and eats with them." In today's Gospel, we hear the lengthiest and most beloved of the three ensuing stories, sometimes called the parable of the Prodigal Son.

But that's a bit of a misnomer, because the story is about two sons. Two sons dishonor the father, one with his actions that set the story in motion, and the other with his reactions to the father's generous open-heartedness when the story takes its turn at the first son's homecoming. Both boys are reprehensible. The scribes and Pharisees might complain about Jesus's table partners, but no more so, one can assume, than his peasant audience complained about the rich and the priests.

Jesus knows that we're all thinking the other guy gets special treatment; the other guy is a worse sinner than us. But we're all fallen: All of us are sinners, and what we see and resent in the behavior of others is often a mirror of what we hate in ourselves. In real life, we are both sons at one time or another, either recalcitrant and greedy like the younger son, or hard-hearted and resentful, like the elder.

What the father seems to want out of all this is simple: two sons. He wants to reconcile the family and live life the way it was meant to be lived. As members of the community of Jesus, attentive to the Gospel, we are summoned to fashion lives that imitate God, who is "kind and merciful" and who sent his son "that all may be one," and has "entrusted the good news of reconciliation to us."

Not everyone is in favor of this agenda. Some religious people don't see universal reconciliation as the will of God. That's not us, though. In Dorothy Day's words, "Heaven is a banquet and life is a banquet, too, even with a crust, where there is companionship."[4] That starts here and now. Step inside the door.

PRACTICE: Has someone opened a door to forgiveness or reconciliation through which you have so far refused to walk? Is someone waiting for you to open that door? Breathe. Release. Open.

THIRD SUNDAY OF LENT
YEAR A: EXODUS 17:3–7; PSALMS 95:1–2, 6–7, 8–9;
ROMANS 5:1–2, 5–8; JOHN 4:5–42

YEAR B: EXODUS 20:1–17; PSALMS 19:8, 9, 10, 11; I
CORINTHIANS 1:22–25; JOHN 2:13–25

YEAR C: EXODUS 3:1–8A, 13–15; PSALMS 103:1–2, 3–4,
6–7, 8, 11; I CORINTHIANS 10:1–6, 10–12; LUKE 13:1–9

Let's take a fresh look at the story of the woman
at the well and what it reveals to us about sin and
grace.

After making a point about the mortal enmity
between Jews and Samaritans, John sets the scene
at Jacob's well, where Jacob met his great love,
Rachel. Then, in the exchange about the husbands,
the woman's version of the story is, "I have no
husband." But Jesus insists, "You are right. You
have had five. The one you have now (that is,
number six) is not your husband." So, six husbands.
In Jewish numerology, she is perfectly incomplete.
But here she is, talking to a man at Jacob's well.

Now remember that the first successful mission of
the apostolic Church was to Samaria, where Philip's
preaching of the Gospel met with great success
(Acts 8). Imagine! After centuries of hatred between
them, the preaching of a Jew about a Jew resulted in
many Samaritans coming to the Way!

In a hostile situation, Jesus speaks from his need.
"Give me a drink." He starts a conversation. He
cracks a window and lets in some air and light.

He unfolds her story gradually. A relationship is forged. The ancient barriers dissolve. She becomes an apostle, inviting neighbors to meet this Jew she met at Jacob's well. Finally, number seven. She's met her (perfect) match.

Today's Gospel isn't about a sinful woman coming to faith. It's about the reconciliation of nations alienated for centuries by hatred and blood. The woman is Samaria. Jesus himself is the water of Jacob's well, and in him enemies are joined in a new relationship. The power of sin is broken.

Do you reject sin? Our cooperation with prejudice and hatred help give social sin its life. It just takes two people, in vulnerability and compassion, to subvert the evil and make a new world possible.

PRAYER: If I hear your voice today, Lord, even in the guise of a stranger or an enemy, at the well of love, open my heart to you. Amen.

MONDAY OF THE THIRD WEEK OF LENT
2 KINGS 5:1–15A; PSALMS 42:2, 3; 43:3, 4; LUKE 4:24–30

For context, read this Gospel story in its entirety, from verse 14 of Luke 4 through verse 30. Jesus, fresh from the Jordan River experience and his desert ordeal, comes to Nazareth on the Sabbath. He reads from the Isaiah scroll in the synagogue, about the arrival of the jubilee in the person of the prophet anointed with the Holy Spirit, and says, "Today, this scripture has been fulfilled in your hearing." The audience radiates approval for Nazareth's favorite son.

Then the sermon continues with today's passage, in which Jesus tells the assembly that freedom from debt, the victory of the poor, and the healing promised by the arrival of God's empire is not only for them, and never has been. He reminds them of the other story we hear today, the healing of Naaman the Syrian by Elisha, and also of the bounty shown by Elijah to a Phoenician woman in another passage. Suddenly the very same crowd, on the very same Sabbath, wants to throw him off a cliff.

Reconciliation is breaking down walls. The structures of sin have been in place for a long time. We imagine that our borders, armies, national interests, laws, and religious sectarianism are necessary aspects of civilization, but the message of Jesus is that all of that needs to be reevaluated. What exists may need to come down so that something new can happen.

Proclaiming the Gospel isn't for filling seats in churches. It's turning toward God in order to find one another. Conversion is learning to act like brothers and sisters, here, in this world, sharing our gifts so that all have, at minimum, enough.

Most of the time, we don't want to throw our preachers off a cliff. But occasionally they hit the right nerve of nationalism or sectarianism. Then we marginalize, persecute, or kill them for their message. You know their names: Bonhoeffer, Ellacuría, Berrigan, Donovan, King, Romero. They're pigeonholed as romantics, disturbers of the peace, or sanctioned as enemies of the state. But they speak with the voice of Christ, and their voices will not be silenced by death.

Joining their number is as simple as rejecting sin, believing in the God of Jesus, and renewing our baptismal promises on Easter.

PRAYER: Lord, all of us are outsiders to you, and yet, while we were still in our sin, you have loved us. Break open the borders of our hearts, and let your unrestricted grace pour through us into the world.

TUESDAY OF THE THIRD WEEK OF LENT
DANIEL 3:25, 34–43; PSALMS 25:4BC–5AB, 6, 7BC, 8–9;
MATTHEW 18:21–35

When the Hebrew Scriptures ask God to "remember" the covenant, to remember Israel, to "remember your mercies," as Psalm 25 does today, it is generally because things are going badly. Israel imagines that God got busy with other things, went on a vacation or took a nap and forgot about them; otherwise things could not be so bad. Or God may have turned away from Israel on account of their sin, so Israel prays, "remember your covenant," which God vowed to Abraham and Moses never to break. If God remembers, things will change. God's "thoughts" are reality.

Azariah (or Abednego, his Babylonian name) stands up in the flaming death-pit ordered for him and his companions by Nebuchadnezzar, and reminds God of how much his sinful clan depends on God, and how God had made promises and delivered them in the past. "Don't let the gods of these conquerors show you up," he is praying. Take care of business. Remember who you are, and remember us. If you remember, things will change.

And Jesus tells a parable about forgetting that we have been forgiven, and the chaos that ensues when we start to act as though the debts owed to us are somehow worse and less forgivable than our own sin. No good can come of it. It begins a cycle of torture and misery from which there is no escape.

When we're asked, "Remember to get some ice at the store," the message isn't simply to think about it, but to actually seek the ice out, buy it, and bring it home. Remembering is integrating what ought to be with what is. Remembering is reconciliation. Remembering God, remembering Jesus, needs to be that kind of remembering.

So let's remember being forgiven. Remember "our Father." Remember "love one another" and "love your enemies" and "take up your cross" and "whoever would be greatest must serve the rest." Remember to forgive as we have been forgiven. The alternative is a world in chaos. But to remember is to share in the act of creation, the very life of God.

Practice: "Forgive us our sins, as we forgive those who are in debt to us." Pray the Lord's Prayer today, and mean it. Remember what you have asked for in the thousands of iterations of that prayer.

WEDNESDAY OF THE THIRD WEEK OF LENT
DEUTERONOMY 4:1, 5–9; PSALMS 147:12–13, 15–16, 19–20; MATTHEW 5:17–19

• DAILY MEDITATIONS FOR LENT •

A.J. Jacobs is an author and freelance writer for *Esquire* magazine. He is Jewish, but as he says, "Jewish in the same way the Olive Garden is an Italian restaurant." His 2008 book, *The Year of Living Biblically,* narrates his attempt to live for a year following every prescription of the Jewish bible. Outrageous as this sounds, what began as a lark ends up being a genuinely religious experience. The experiment led him to a profound sense of gratitude and of sacredness. Summarizing his year, he wrote, "I thought religion would make me live with my head in the clouds, but as often as not, it grounds me in this world."

The "laws and statutes of the Lord" spoken of in Deuteronomy are a source of life. Not a word of the law or the prophets will pass away. Yet we know from elsewhere in the Gospel that Jesus had a specific approach and attitude toward the law that was guided by his experience of God. Jesus took issue with the way other Pharisees applied and enforced the law with such rigidity, especially when their behavior was hypocritical and not guided by compassion.

53

Jesus says that he came to "fulfill the law and the prophets." Like other prophets, he saw that the heart of the law was not merely a set of regulations and restrictions but a way of opening us up to life shared with other people, making us aware of our equal importance as children of God. Law also admonishes us to keep doing the right thing even when we don't feel like it, putting an objective reality in the path of our runaway desire, sense of entitlement, or personal preference. Law is good, the prophets would say, as long as it doesn't replace God. Ultimately, "it is mercy that I desire, not sacrifice."

As A.J. Jacobs wrote in *The Year of Living Biblically,* "It is easier to act yourself into a new way of thinking than it is to think yourself into a new way of acting."

PRAYER: "Praise the LORD! / How good it is to sing praises to our God; / for he is gracious, and a song of praise is fitting" (Psalms 147:1). Amen.

THURSDAY OF THE THIRD WEEK OF LENT
JEREMIAH 7:23–28; PSALMS 95:1–2, 6–7, 8–9; LUKE 11:14–23

Release from slavery isn't an easy thing. The foundational scriptural metaphor for it is the Exodus, a thirsty, forty-year march through the desert, looking for a land flowing with milk and honey—which, when finally discovered, already has someone living in it. In its infamous nadir at the rock of Meribah, where the Israelites grumbled to Moses that they were better off as slaves than as free people, the whole journey nearly collapses.

The journey of discipleship to the Promised Land of the reign of God is no easier. It is not a place to which we can go alone, nor can we thrive without a community around us. Turning toward the reign of God and away from the self-interest of lesser gods requires a group formed by determined love, one that knows its center even as it invites everyone into its peaceful, expansive borders.

Life in the world, that is, wherever the values of the kingdom are not lived, will inevitably show its violent heart, and may be an occasion for conversion to the Gospel. But the Christian community should not delude itself that it can run like Caesar's world, or rule this world with Caesar's law. The reign of God is not a place of violence, threat, and enforced allegiance, but of hospitality, service, equality, and justice. Its law is *agape*.

Our hearts may have been seduced by our well-defended borders, our stealth weapons, tax shelters, and gated communities. But these kinds of structures are built on the backs of the poor. They prevent us from experiencing the pain of others. They numb our compassion. They are false security, because they do not contribute to the well-being of everyone.

Christ comes into our world again, every Lent, to drive out the demons that have muted the Gospel. Christ sees us, captives in the house of darkness. Strong as it is, he enters to overcome its defender with the word of life.

PRACTICE: Can you be someone's release from slavery today? Sometimes all it takes is to let someone know that they're not alone. Or it may be more: changing to fair trade items, or paying more for sustainably grown food. Remember that everyone matters, the same as you, the same as Christ, all the time.

FRIDAY OF THE THIRD WEEK OF LENT
HOSEA 14:2–10; PSALMS 81:6C–8A, 8BC–9, 10–11AB, 14, 17; MARK 12:28B–34

My friend and mentor, the late Fr. Jim Dunning, told a story that he recorded in his book *Echoing God's Word* that sheds a little light on today's Scripture. He said that he once traveled to Australia to give a presentation to clergy. The priest who met him at Sydney airport introduced himself and hurried him out to the car. They were running a few minutes late, he said, telling Jim, "Toss your port in my boot, and we'll be on the way." Jim said he was perplexed for a minute, but didn't want to seem like the ugly

American, so he poured his wine in the man's shoe, and got in his car.

For most of us, language seems simple and transparent. I say "tree," you know what I'm talking about. But in truth, words are symbols of internal realities, and the less concrete the reality they represent, the more slippery their meaning becomes. Bill Clinton, remember, famously argued, "It depends on what the meaning of the word *is* is." "To be," or "is," is a pretty slippery concept. So is the concept of "God."

All of us, pretty much, love some god, or combination of gods, with our whole mind, soul, heart, and strength. What we often enough don't deal with, what we don't practice remembering, is who the specific God is whom the Holy Spirit reveals through the ministry of Jesus and the witness of Scripture. When we repeat our baptismal promises, even when we simply speak to one another about "God," we may be saying, hearing, and meaning different things, like the port and the boot in Jim Dunning's story. How can we discern the truth of our belief?

Today's Gospel suggests a path to discernment: "The second is like it. Love your neighbor as yourself." To the extent that our faith in God leads us to treat our neighbor like our self, or like "one of the family," we believe in the God whom Jesus, and our baptismal promises and the Creed, calls "Father."

PRACTICE: Consider this: Do you believe in God, the Father Almighty, Creator of heaven and earth? What does that mean to you?

SATURDAY OF THE THIRD WEEK OF LENT
HOSEA 6:1–6; PSALMS 51:3–4, 18–19, 20–21AB; LUKE 18:9–14

It is fairly rare in the Church's liturgy that the antiphon (the people's part) of the Responsorial Psalm is not taken from the text of the psalm itself. Today's use of Psalm 51 is one example of a departure from this practice, as the lectionary takes the Hosea text, "It is mercy (*hesed*) that I desire, not sacrifice."

Look at the structure of the First Reading. The first voice is Israel, ostensibly repenting in the face of some national disaster. "Things are bad, but God always comes through. Let's try to do what God wants. Then things will be all right." But God responds sternly, looking for action more than prayer. "Your loyalty (*hesed*) is like the dew...but I want a different loyalty, and not empty words and rites. Knowledge of God, rather than burnt offerings." The structure of the Hebrew implies equality between *hesed* and knowledge of God. Also, *hesed* is generally translated as loving-kindness, or mercy. Here it is seen as the heart of the covenant itself, and the true perception of who God is and what God does.

The Pharisee in the parable today is like Israel in the Hosea text. He assumes that God loves him, and that he can depend on his prayers being answered, because he keeps the covenant as he understands it, a complex set of laws and rites that render him clean. The tax collector has no such illusions. He knows that God is God and that he is not, and nothing he can do can change God's mind about anything. His only prayer is, "*Hesed*, Lord, *hesed*."

To be like God is to act like God. To act like God

is to show *hesed* toward the other, in fact, the call is greatest to show *hesed* toward the one who, like Israel, doesn't deserve it, who is a recidivist offender and part-time lover. To at least know what the tax collector knew is enough, Jesus says. The tax collector *did* nothing, but went home justified.

Do you believe in God? The first step may be in just admitting that we are not God, and letting that knowledge govern our actions with others, inside and outside of the temple.

PRAYER: Lord, be merciful to me, a sinner. Amen.

FOURTH SUNDAY OF LENT

YEAR A: 1 SAMUEL 16:1B, 6–7, 10–13; PSALMS 23:1–3A, 3B–4, 5, 6; EPHESIANS 5:8–14; JOHN 9:1–41

YEAR B: 2 CHRONICLES 36:14–16, 19–23; PSALMS 137:1–2, 3, 4–5, 6; EPHESIANS 2:4–10; JOHN 3:14–21

YEAR C: JOSHUA 5:9A, 10–12; PSALMS 34:2–3, 4–5, 6–7; 2 CORINTHIANS 5:17–21; LUKE 15:1–3, 11–32

What did we hear yesterday? "I desire mercy, not sacrifice." Believers who take pride in ritual are at risk of substituting rite for lived faith. It stands to reason that one of the scrutinies might be called upon to remind us of that as we pray with the elect and gradually introduce them to the mystery of grace and sin.

John drops a detail early into the story of the man born blind that "Jesus had made the clay and opened his eyes on a Sabbath." Without that detail, we wouldn't have a story. With it, Jesus's enemies seize an opportunity to make a case for blasphemy, because no one could claim to be from God and at the same time break the laws of Sabbath rest. If they could prove this one, they'd have Jesus in chains.

But Jesus doesn't just know about God, he knows God. "The Father and I are one," he will say, and he knows that he is God's beloved. He sees the disconnection between the blind man's plight and the God of the temple. He can't imagine a God who could heal a man today but waits until tomorrow to do it. But between the man and healing loom the chaos of social sin and the arrogant human mechanisms that pretend to control the flow of grace. So Jesus employs a bit of scriptural street theater: He bends down and makes clay with spittle and earth, spreads it on the man's eyes, and tells him to go to the pool and wash it off. "And there was light." Creation happens, in broad daylight.

Do you believe in God? Which God? The one who insists that we enforce strictures that further enfeeble the marginalized and distraught, or the one who will not wait until tomorrow to brighten our world? The second scrutiny sits in judgment today upon the blindness that adamantly closes its eyes. It encourages in us a new vision, the sight of a God who sees not as we see, but who looks beyond appearance to the heart.

PRAYER: Be my vision, O Lord of my heart. Amen.

MONDAY OF THE FOURTH WEEK OF LENT
ISAIAH 65:17–21; PSALMS 30:2, 4, 5–6, 11–12A, 13B;
JOHN 4:43–54

Though we often tend to hear Scripture in person-alistic and spiritual ways, every page of it is steeped in the political situation of Israel in specific times and places. The transformative promise we hear in Isaiah today is spoken about the cosmos even as its word of hope is directed toward a ruined Jerusalem: "I am about to create new heavens and a new earth." Sorrow will be banished, and the grief caused by death will be no more.

As we move deeper into Lent and closer to the sacramental dying and rising of the baptismal rites, our reflections approach ever nearer the heart of the paschal mystery: the God who creates life, sustains life, and agitates for life wherever and whenever other gods interfere. Jesus is God's great agitator for life, whose word and ministry, life, death, and resurrection point the way toward a different civilization, one not based on violence and greed but upon a foundation of justice and equality. These flow from the worship and imitation of a God who is like a father, who wants a world in constructive relationship.

The world that we've made is too much a place of sickness and death. Sickness is too often a result of poverty and neglect, a side effect of hunger and pollution. While we may not have control over the progress and origin of disease, we can exercise some control of the power it has over people, especially the very young and the elderly, by agitating for life like Jesus did.

We can work to end poverty, neglect, hunger, pollution, war, and the many other human institutions that perpetuate and engender sickness and death. We can do this by advocacy, by voting, by almsgiving, and by ongoing targeted sacrificial giving of our goods. Lent is a time we get back into those practices if we've let them slide. Today is a good day to think about all that. "Now is the day of salvation."

PRACTICE: Reevaluate your almsgiving for Lent and sacrificial giving in general. Make a plan to contribute, if you can, to the healing, reparative work of Catholic Relief Services or Catholic Charities.

TUESDAY OF THE FOURTH WEEK OF LENT
EZEKIEL 47:1–9, 12; PSALMS 46:2–3, 5–6, 8–9; JOHN 5:1–3A, 5–16

"Do you want to be well?" What a strange question to ask a cripple, laying alongside other cripples, waiting for hope to come bubbling up out of the water, frustrated over and over by his body's inability to respond to the promise of healing. What an overflow of gratitude that the healer chanced to come by today, saw his predicament, and said, "It's over now. Pick up your mat and go home."

The startling vision of Ezekiel of a wide, fertile river pouring out of the right side of the renewed Jerusalem Temple offered hope to those who had been led into exile, seen their city laid waste, and their king deposed and humiliated. The water from that river would be a life source to the whole land. In prophetic language, those who hope for restoration and abundant life should look to the God who made a home within the Temple. Today's Psalm iterates that refrain: "The Lord of Hosts is with us, our stronghold is the God of Jacob."

Jesus delivers that restoration and life in his own person. Full of the Spirit, he offers to everyone the choice for a different God, and announces the arrival of the promised jubilee in the gentle reign of his Father. Healing the crippled man by the pool of Bethesda, Jesus demonstrates the bounty of a God who works both inside and outside human structures. We have not heard the end of this story: The holders of the purse strings of grace are by no means convinced of the prophet's origin or designs.

Do you believe in Jesus Christ, God's only son, our Lord? Jesus proclaims God's favor for everyone, both inside and outside our communities and structures that mediate membership and grace. Belief in Christ will be an adventure, perhaps a dangerous one. In baptism, we make a leap of faith, and literally take the plunge into the river of life.

PRACTICE: Drink a glass of water today intentionally. Linger over it. Think of the life and health it brings to you, and that it has brought on its journey to your life. Let the presence of God in the water speak to you with healing and integrity.

WEDNESDAY OF THE FOURTH WEEK OF LENT
ISAIAH 49:8–15; PSALMS 145:8–9, 13CD–14, 17–18;
JOHN 5:17–30

Cultural anthropologist René Girard describes human beings as mimetic creatures; that is, we learn how to be human, take care of ourselves, and live as a family by watching how other people do it. Girard made his name by describing a theory of mimetic violence, by which he means that we see what other people want, and see that it has goodness to it, and so we want it for ourselves. This leads to violence and rivalry between groups.

He describes the rise of religion as a way of temporarily escaping this cycle by means of the scapegoat mechanism, whereby the group transfers the need for murder and violence to an individual or individuals. The group leaders bless the ouster or death of the scapegoat, returning the group to a kind of peace. Then the cycle of mimesis, or coveting desire for the same goods, begins again. Mimetic desire fuels civilization.

Girard is a Catholic, and sees the death and resurrection of Jesus as the beginning of the end, a kind of divine covert operation begun to expose the scapegoat mechanism for what it is. The scapegoat, innocent (or no more guilty than the group), is put to death or ostracized to please the deity. The death of Jesus exposes the lie of this. Jesus is innocent, and his death is an affront to the God of life, who raises him from death, nonviolently overcoming his killers.

Girard and his followers describe the path of reversal for mimetic desire as imitating God, who lets the rain fall and sun shine on good and bad alike. Be like God, they might say, who only wants good for the other, rather than for oneself. Jesus does only "what he sees the Father doing." If we could choose the way of Jesus, the peaceable kingdom would be right before our eyes.

PRAYER: Lord, let me imitate you as you imitate the Father. Teach me to love my enemies, and to love without counting the cost. Amen.

THURSDAY OF THE FOURTH WEEK OF LENT
EXODUS 32:7–14; PSALMS 106:19–20, 21–22, 23; JOHN 5:31–47

Today's First Reading describes the fortieth day of the first of three successive forty-day retreats Moses makes on Mount Horeb to be with God. And we think Lent is long!

The First Reading and Psalm today recount and celebrate Moses's advocacy for Israel when God wanted to destroy it for building and worshiping a golden calf. Interestingly, it is not the image of a false god that got Israel into trouble. It was that they made an image, as Aaron says, of the God "who brought you out of Egypt." They had made an image of their own God, unfortunately, just after they had been told that they should make no graven images.

Aren't some of our false gods really just our own idolatrous versions of the one who called us to be a people?

Like the story of Abraham bargaining with God over the destruction of Sodom and Gomorrah (Genesis 18: 16–33), this narrative's enduring feature is that Moses takes the side of his stiff-necked and sinful people before God, who wants to destroy them. In the end, God relents.

Jesus continues to reprove those Jewish leaders who took issue with his healing of the crippled man on the Sabbath. Moses went before God and pled the case of his people when he knew they were sinners. Moses, the prophet of God, took the part of the people against God. Why were these religious leaders using the Torah to attack the healing of one of the weakest of Israel's children? You do not have the love of God in you, Jesus warns, and "your accuser is Moses."

PRACTICE: Revisit intercessory prayer. Remembering yesterday's Scriptures, pray for your enemies and competitors today. If you pray for a good outcome for everyone, at least you're beginning to align your will with God's.

FRIDAY OF THE FOURTH WEEK OF LENT
WISDOM 2:1A, 12–22; PSALMS 34:17–18, 19–20, 21, 23; JOHN 7:1–2, 10, 25–30

Deciding for the reign of God is a matter of life and death. To make the choice that Jesus lays before us, opting for God's kingdom over Caesar's, is to choose a path of treason. Scripture uses many synonyms to describe the reign of the god Caesar, notably "the kingdom of this world," along with metaphors like "darkness," "night," and even "death" to suggest its meaning. The reign of God, or the "kingdom of heaven," or "my Father's house" is a world of light, life, and truth.

The choice is daunting and can seem lonely. Those who opt for the reign of God begin to see the world for what it is, and know that to turn toward the Gospel will put them in conflict with the ruling powers. They might be ignored for a while, right up until they begin to expose the death underneath the everyday economy of the world.

Most of the public ministry of Jesus—his teaching and healing and his calling of disciples—took place in Galilee, far away from Jerusalem, home of the Temple priesthood and the Roman governor and his occupying forces. The Gospel says he "went about in Galilee," because in Judea the elite knew enough about him that "they were looking for an opportunity to kill him."

When we think about the implications of belief in Christ and the reign of God, we can be overwhelmed. Our natural tendency is to stay in Galilee, practice living in the reign of God with like-minded people, and try, to borrow a phrase used by Walter Willimon and Stanley Hauerwas, to find a way to live in this or any nation as "resident aliens in the Christian colony."[5]

Ultimately, though, we will either set our eyes on Jerusalem, or like Dr. King, Archbishop Romero, Dietrich Bonhoeffer, and their Lord before them, Jerusalem will find us. "You who were baptized with Christ Jesus were baptized into his death," St. Paul wrote to the Romans. Ultimately, Jerusalem is our destiny, and the journey takes a community.

PRACTICE: Where is that danger zone for you, the place where you know that living the Gospel will cost you your life as it is? Can you set a goal to move in that direction? Whom do you need to travel with you?

SATURDAY OF THE FOURTH WEEK OF LENT
JEREMIAH 11:18–20; PSALMS 7:2–3, 9BC–10, 11–12;
JOHN 7:40–53

An occupational hazard of any faith is the sense that we have God figured out. We make judgments based on our faith and on Scripture, tradition, and practice, and we assume that we are making those judgments the way God wants us to make them. Over time, we can get to a place at which we think we have God figured out. The chief priests and Pharisees tried to enforce the parameters of the law as they saw it. They thought they knew what the messiah, or "Christ," would look like when he came, where he would be from and what he would do.

Assuming we know God's ways can lead us

absurdly astray, as when a minister every few years predicts the end of the world based on the word of the Lord, or when a sect equates some natural disaster or man-made horror to be God's specific punishment for a sin that that sect's leaders find particularly abhorrent. Or it can take more subtle form, as when the Church enshrines its tradition on so high an altar that new information from science, that Galilee from whence no prophet can arise, is rejected out of hand as being false teaching. Galileo, as it were, from Galilee.

The "no prophet can come from Galilee" perspective is inherently ironic, since the scholars of the law who made the claim overlooked the prophet Jonah (and possibly Nahum) in their judgment. Prophets come from wherever God calls them, and God doesn't always call them from expected places. The prophetic calling is to judge mainstream faith. One can hardly imagine that kind of judgment always arising organically from within the mainstream itself. In Einstein's famous dictum, "We cannot solve our problems with the same thinking we used when we created them."[6]

The baptismal promises call us to faith in the Holy Spirit, who "has spoken through the prophets." Even the Church's vision is the vision of people, and "the LORD does not see as mortals see. They look on the outward appearance, but the LORD looks on the heart." (1 Samuel 16:7) Humility and compassion will help us clear our vision.

PRAYER: Teach me *your* ways, Lord. Guide me by *your* light. Lead and I will follow.

FIFTH SUNDAY OF LENT

YEAR A: EZEKIEL 37:12–14; PSALMS 130:1–2, 3–4, 5–6, 7–8; ROMANS 8:8–11; JOHN 11:1–45

YEAR B: JEREMIAH 31:31–34; PSALMS 51:3–4, 12–13, 14–15; HEBREWS 5:7–9; JOHN 12:20–33

YEAR C: ISAIAH 43:16–21; PSALMS 126:1–2A, 2B–3, 4–5, 6; PHILIPPIANS 3:8–14; JOHN 8:1–11

If we see, as John Dominic Crossan suggests, the campaign of Jesus during his ministry as offering an alternative empire of "peace through justice" to the violent empire of the Roman god, Caesar, we get a new context for today's Gospel and scrutiny.[7] There is no more fearsome weapon in the arsenal of any Caesar in any era than death, no more persuasive strategy than torture and threat of death.

In order to persuade anyone to choose Abba rather than Caesar as God, one must show a power stronger than death. At the tomb of Lazarus, Jesus groans with emotion as he prepares to do battle.

The fear of death, or the delusion that we can escape it, or the attempt to narcotize ourselves against it, governs so many of our choices. Death is a shadow over how we spend our time and money. In biblical language, death determines who it is that we love with our whole heart, soul, mind, and strength. Civilization is glued together by threats of death and violence. Christ offers an alternative: God as father, peace through justice, equality in the family. Which God will we follow? Following one means turning our back on the other.

My friend, Tom O'Hern, runs a small NGO in the middle of Korogocho, a slum in Nairobi that is home to a million people. A million people! Think of it. Tom has told me how these people suffer from systemic poverty resulting from government corruption. They are plagued by violence, drug use, and HIV/AIDS. They live in the utter hopelessness that is death. They see no escape from their situation. Tom's ministry has been to organize small esteem-building groups, soccer teams, small savings groups, and micro-businesses to give them a glimmer of hope. Korogocho is a tomb. Tom is like Christ, shouting at the doorway: "Come out of there!"

PRACTICE: Consider making Family Hope Charity, Tom's group in Korogocho, part of your Lenten almsgiving. Visit www.familyhopecharity.org for information on donating. Or choose another organization that can use your help.

MONDAY OF THE FIFTH WEEK OF LENT
DANIEL 13:1–9, 15–17, 19–30, 33–62; PSALMS 23:1–3A,
3B–4, 5, 6; JOHN 8:1–11

If the Church were taking an opportunity to include a warning about the sins of the flesh in this season, this would be the day. In a passion-length passage from Daniel, we have a cautionary tale about the dreadful gravity of lust; the Gospel story crackles with the mortal panic of a woman caught in the act of adultery and facing stoning at the hands of a brutal mob. But by the end of either passage, and certainly from the confident gratitude of Psalm 23, it is clear that today's Scripture is not concerned with sexual sin at all, or, at most, only in a tertiary way as a catalyst for worse human action.

What we do hear today is a warning against false condemnation, and a divine voice whispering, "Do not be afraid" to those unjustly accused by the powerful. In both readings, high-ranking men accuse women, one innocent, one possibly less so, in order to get what they want. In both cases, the judgment of God is on the side of the accused, who is restored to life in the community. The men in Daniel do not fare well; the accusers in the Gospel lose only their honor and their scapegoat. In confronting Christ, they discover the truth about themselves.

Echoing yesterday's third scrutiny, the faith lesson here is about God's ultimate power over death. The

Father raised Jesus from death to vindicate his life, simultaneously exposing the corruption and impotence of the systems that killed him, and proving, without a single vindictive blow, that the worst the god Caesar can do, terrible as it may be, cannot overcome the God of life.

"Sin no more," says Jesus to all of us. Believe in my God if you really want to live.

PRACTICE: Do you believe in the forgiveness of sin, the resurrection of the body, and life everlasting?

TUESDAY OF THE FIFTH WEEK OF LENT
NUMBERS 21:4–9; PSALMS 102:2–3, 16–18, 19–21;
JOHN 8:21–30

It's a great story, the Exodus, but who can blame the poor Israelites for complaining? All those years wandering in the desert, often with nothing to eat but manna. The diet was wearing a little thin. In response to their ingratitude, God sends poisonous snakes into their camp, and they are beset until

Moses hoists a bronze serpent. Those who looked at it would be saved.

Jesus lifted up on the cross would save us as well, so the Church saw in Moses's serpent a metaphor for the crucified Christ. But crucifixion, in the first and second centuries C.E., was no metaphor. It was a horrific reality, one repeated thousands of times throughout the Roman Empire, as the forces of Caesar demonstrated the power of the *Pax Romana* by imposing a death sentence on insurgents and other enemies of the state. For Rome, lifting up on the cross was a warning: If you do likewise, this will be you.

When fourteen-year-old Emmett Till was murdered in 1955 by two white men for allegedly ogling a white woman, his mother insisted on an open-casket funeral because she "wanted the world to see what they did to my baby."[8] Her brave action rallied black support and white sympathizers, galvanizing the civil rights movement. Similarly, the parents of young Sandy Hook victim Noah Pozner did the same, calling attention to the issues of gun violence and gun-control legislation.

When we look upon Christ crucified, we see the truth of us, both our own mortality and the horrors of which we're capable of inflicting on others when the violence within erupts to the surface. The message of Jesus led inexorably and inevitably to his death at the hands of Rome, but God raised him from death, validating his life, words, and work, including his "blasphemous" claim that he was doing the Father's work.

May the paschal mystery give us courage to look at who we are and how we harm one another, and turn toward Jesus and the Father.

PRACTICE: Do you believe in Jesus Christ, who suffered under Pontius Pilate, was crucified, died, and was buried?

WEDNESDAY OF THE FIFTH WEEK OF LENT
DANIEL 3:14–20, 91–92, 95; DANIEL 3:52, 53, 54, 55, 56; JOHN 8:31–42

The choice between kingdoms, as we have seen, is carried by many opposites in John: light and darkness, freedom and slavery, life and death, above and below. For the evangelists and their communities, who are making meaning in their lives through their experience of Jesus, the choice is stark. It is always phrased in these diametrical oppositions. In John's Gospel, Jesus also uses the word *truth* to describe the reign of God. Today, Jesus promises that those who believe in him know the truth, and the truth will set them free.

The three young men in the book of Daniel have a clear choice of gods before them, too. One was a huge golden idol made by the Babylonian king Nebuchadnezzar. The other was the God of Israel. Failure to choose Nebuchadnezzar's god meant death by fire. The choice doesn't get much clearer than that.

But it is rarely so simple for us, is it? For centuries now, we have imagined a kind of détente that began with Constantine, who married the Roman Empire to the Church and gave the Church the kind of political power that before had only been used against it. Flags and crosses have gotten so tangled up in meaning that Christians can wage war against other Christians, making widows and orphans instead of helping them. That's not to mention the way we treat non-Christians, whom we have also been commanded to love as we love ourselves. We bless our weapons. Religious institutions invest in corporations that exploit people and the environment. We throw around words such as *evildoers* to describe people who are enemies of our state.

It is not easy to disentangle from this morass. We're involved in systemic sin and evil in ways of which we're not even aware. But it's still sin; it's the works and empty promises of the Lie. I'm involved in it. I don't see a way out, but I look to the Gospel for truth and light, and for a community with whom I can turn once and for all toward the freedom of God's children won by Jesus and given to me in baptism.

PRACTICE: Do you reject sin so as to live in the freedom of God's children?

THURSDAY OF THE FIFTH WEEK OF LENT
GENESIS 17:3–9; PSALMS 105:4–5, 6–7, 8–9; JOHN
8:51–59

The covenant with Abraham unfolds throughout
the story of Israel, a story of judges, kings, conquest
and subjugation, true worship and syncretism.
Through it all, "God remembers his covenant."
People forget, but God remembers. When things
go poorly for the nation, Israel blames itself, or
imagines God has turned away or gone to sleep and
needs to be awakened by prayer and noisy supplica-
tion in order to pay attention again.

"I will be your God, you will be my people." This
covenant was never between equals. It was never
going to be possible for the human community to
be the people of God, formed by the love of justice
and mercy as enshrined in God's Word. Somehow,
we just can't keep faith with each other. We can't
act with integrity in business. We amass wealth at
the expense of the unwary and weak. We cut our
losses by ignoring the needs of the sick, poor, and

yes, errant, who can't carry their own weight. We set up structures that enable our bad behavior and rewrite our creeds to make allowances for our greed and violence.

Prophets are sent to expose our sinfulness for what it is. They forbid us from seeing our idols and illusions of piety as doxology. We don't want to hear from them. The more we have invested our lives in our false gods and deviant practices, the more we need the prophets marginalized or dead.

Enter Jesus, a human being like us, and yet, somehow, the Son of God. Finally, humanity has a champion. Jesus not only keeps the covenant and shows a way of faithfulness to God that has the awful clarity of life and death, but he *is* the covenant. In Jesus, the presence of the living God infuses and inspires human activity. Jesus invites us into the Way, which, by the indwelling of God's own Holy Spirit in us, allows us to share in the life and mission of God. And yet, the very idea that this could be engenders a murderous rage in keepers of the status quo.

PRACTICE: Do you believe in "Jesus Christ, his only son, our Lord"?

FRIDAY OF THE FIFTH WEEK OF LENT
JEREMIAH 20:10–13; PSALMS 18:2–3A, 3BC–4, 5–6, 7; JOHN 10:31–42

These days approaching Holy Week are drenched in the sweat of dread and impending doom. Lent began with a prophet (Joel) announcing some portent of plague or invasion that might be avoided if the whole nation, from king to priest to nursing mothers and newlyweds, repented and turned back to God. They did repent, and God did relent.

Today, five weeks later, the prophet Jeremiah, announcing another imminent disaster, cries out to God for rescue from the enemies his prophecy has made him. Jeremiah cries out in gratitude, too, for God has "rescued the life of the poor from the power of the wicked."

Jesus claims, just before today's Gospel verses, that "the Father and I are one." This precipitates our opening verse, "The Jews (again) picked up rocks to stone Jesus." It's beginning to sound like a refrain, even in the more serene narrative of John. Things are spinning out of control. The special relationship that Jesus claims to God, a relationship that he says is validated by the signs he works and that gives authority to his words, is a problem for some of his hearers in spite of the signs. The situation has heated up to a point that Jesus feels the need to retreat to the Judean wilderness.

What is the lesson here for us as we approach the Easter waters? It may be that the suffering and death of Jesus did not replace whatever suffering or death might be in store for us for the sake of the Gospel and the mission of the Father. "No servant is greater than the master," and the suffering inflicted on the master will be, and certainly has been, inflicted on those who follow.

But the suffering and death of Jesus, caught up in the paschal mystery, reveal to us that God will "rescue the life of the poor." God is, in the words of Psalm 18, "strength, rock, fortress, and deliverer." To choose Christ is to choose the cross. But to choose the cross is to share in the resurrection.

"If we die with him, we shall also live with him." Let that faith sustain us through the days ahead to the paschal feast.

PRAYER: When faced with the possibility of suffering for the sake of the Gospel, Lord, give me strength to face it with courage. But, in your mercy, do not lead me into that trial, but deliver me.

SATURDAY OF THE FIFTH WEEK OF LENT
EZEKIEL 37:21–28; JEREMIAH 31:10, 11–12, 13; JOHN 11:45–57

Everyday folks who observed Jesus generally had a good idea what he was up to. When Jesus asked the apostles, "Who are people saying that I am?" they respond to him that people think he's John or one of the other prophets come back from the dead. They see, in other words, that he is a prophet, one who speaks the word of God fearlessly to the powerful, no matter the personal cost. He's not just a teacher or wonder-worker. He is a prophet.

When Jesus redirects the question to his inner circle, they respond differently. Peter says that Jesus is the Messiah, and Jesus immediately silences him. *Messiah* was a loaded word. In the sense Peter meant it, and as the disciples understood it, *Messiah* engendered the expectation of an imminent political restoration for Israel, and that there might therefore be important leadership positions doled out among the twelve.

Jesus had come to see the anointing of God's Spirit as something different from a call to power. Peter said "Messiah, son of the living God," and meant "king, restorer of Israel." Jesus knew messiah to be Isaiah's suffering servant, beloved son of Abba. As such, he invited us to peacefully reimagine the world around the image of God as "our Father."

Caiaphas, in making the decision to find a way to kill Jesus, inadvertently prophesied the meaning of his death. Jesus was going to die for the nation, and not only for the nation, but also to gather into one the dispersed children of God. The only life that the Messiah's revolution would take was his own, and its purpose was not to be the violent rise of Israel, but the peaceful reconciliation of all people and all nations.

Here we are, two thousand years later, and we have a checkered past as a reconciling community. Caesar and other gods still demand our allegiance with a seduction and vehemence that the Gospel refuses to employ. The Father's mission, entrusted to Jesus and now to us, is unfinished. Our continued participation will be formally requested in just eight days.

PRACTICE: As Holy Week draws near, spend some time reflecting on how your Lenten prayer and practice has prepared you to walk the path of Jesus's passion this week.

PALM SUNDAY OF THE LORD'S PASSION

YEAR A: MATTHEW 21:1–11; ISAIAH 50:4–7; PSALMS
22:8–9 17–18, 19–20, 23–24; PHILIPPIANS 2:6–11;
MATTHEW 26:14—27:66

YEAR B: MARK 11:1–10 OR JOHN 12:12–16; ISAIAH
50:4–7; PSALMS 22:8–9 17–18, 19–20, 23–24;
PHILIPPIANS 2:6–11; MARK 14:1—15:47

YEAR C: LUKE 19:28–40; ISAIAH 50:4–7; PSALMS 22:8–9
17–18, 19–20, 23–24; PHILIPPIANS 2:6–11; LUKE
22:14—23:56

We need to see the political theater that plays out in
the Gospel as the crowd begins to make its way into
the Holy City for Passover. The drama is this: there
are two processions entering Jerusalem on this day.
One is the procession of the Roman governor and
his accompanying legions entering from Caesarea
Maritima to garrison at Herod's palace to keep the
peace during the volatile festival. Caesar's legions
would arrive armed and on horseback, their scarlet
might a warning to any zealots who might want
to start an uprising during the freedom festival of
Passover.

Into another gate would ride the herald of the other God, the prophet Jesus, riding on a donkey, a symbol of agrarian peace. Ignoring threats to his freedom and his life, he comes into Jerusalem to celebrate the Passover with his disciples, but he makes a sign of it by acting as the peaceful "king riding upon an ass" in Zechariah. By his entry, in other words, he offers a different kind of peace and another God, other than the one Pilate represents. He thus makes visible the choice he has offered since he appeared in the Galilean wilderness, a choice between gods and kingdoms: peace through violence, or peace through justice.

In doing so, he eschews the vision of a god whose sacramental signs are warhorses, legions, and weapons. He proclaims a God who is Father, who gathers at table, who is the Lord of life, and who has power over the grave ruled by Caesar. As the Church came to believe that Jesus was the preexisting *Logos* who dwelt with God from the beginning, Paul would make the startling claim that being God did not bind Christ to heaven, but that he poured divinity out and became a servant, enduring death on a cross.

PRACTICE: The days ahead will lead us to the crisis at the heart of the Gospel. Which parade will we choose? Whose God will we worship with our lives?

MONDAY OF HOLY WEEK
ISAIAH 42:1–7; PSALMS 27:1, 2, 3, 13–14; JOHN 12:1–11

The First Reading comes from the first "Servant Song" in the book of the prophet Isaiah; Tuesday and Wednesday we will hear the second and third, and Friday the fourth. These oracles describe a person, group, or nation chosen for "the victory of justice," which is to say for the peaceful implementation of the reign of God.

The Servant is not a conqueror, judge, or ruler in any traditional sense. In fact, suffering is part of the Servant's calling and destiny, as the fourth song reveals. Certainly the early Church and evangelists interpreted the life and ministry of Jesus in the light of these canticles, and there is reason to believe that Jesus's self-identity, revealed in his healings, exorcisms, actions (like washing feet at table), and teaching was somehow deeply influenced by these writings.

"I have called you," God says to the servant, to be covenant, light, vision, and freedom. The Servant is the arrival of the jubilee of God for the whole world. In the Servant, God's presence arrives tangibly and for the benefit of all, particularly those who are debilitated or in distress. Earlier in Lent, we heard Jesus read from the Isaiah scroll at Nazareth, and announce that the prophet's words are "fulfilled in your hearing."

Baptism calls us into union with Christ, the Servant. The mantle of that mission, whose promise is full of God's presence even as it foresees the suffering that awaits the prophet, is laid upon us like the white garment of baptism.

"The Lord is my light and my salvation" when we live like Jesus who did not come to be served but to serve, who rejected any hint of violence or the sword and silenced even the mention of a political kingdom. "The Lord is my light and my salvation" when we believe in a God who calls us to a life of service and witness to God's mission of reconciliation. "The Lord is my light and my salvation" because God is always true to the covenant, and will not allow the Servant's life to be lost forever.

PRAYER: You are my light and my salvation, O Lord. I reject the darkness and walk in your way, this day and every day. Amen.

TUESDAY OF HOLY WEEK
ISAIAH 49:1–6; PSALMS 71:1–2, 3–4A, 5–6AB, 15, 17;
JOHN 13:21–33, 36–38

Peaceable but fraught with intimations of danger, the Gospel is transparent about the cost of discipleship. There is a thread of subversion that even goes through the parables. I'm talking about how parables use images such as yeast "corrupting" bread dough, weeds sown in a field, a thief binding a householder, and even, in the Gospel of Thomas, an assassin's knife.

In today's third Servant Song, the Servant is a concealed weapon, a particularly sleek arrow hidden in the quiver. I hear all of these images not as images of violence but of subversion, as sort of double negatives. The tactic God uses to undermine the world isn't a frontal assault, but subversion. A little yeast in this big ball of corruption will change it completely; God's rescue will come like a thief in the night to take back what the evil one has stolen.

This is comforting, because as numerous as Christians are, it is a lonely task to confront political and religious forces that are satisfied with the distribution of power and wealth in the world. We have become so inured to poverty, corruption, and sin that we're willing to imagine that they are God's will, and so we allow the poor to keep suffering. From their point of view, isn't this betrayal?

It must have been a blow to Jesus that one of the twelve, the inner circle of his companions, had gone over to the Temple authorities offering to hand Jesus over to them away from the Passover crowds. Jesus is the light of the world, but after Judas left the table, "it was night."

The mission of the Servant is planted on our hearts, relentlessly calling us to action. The light that the Servant community bears in the name of the Messiah is a light to the nations. What is about to take place on Calvary and in Jerusalem will change the world. Baptism will make a secret weapon of us, too, if we stand in God's light, and live for the voice that calls us to this mission, and prepared us from our mother's womb.

PRACTICE: Do you reject the glamour of evil, and refuse to be mastered by sin?

WEDNESDAY OF HOLY WEEK
ISAIAH 50:4–9A; PSALMS 69:8–10, 21–22, 31, 33–34; MATTHEW 26:14–25

Today is "Spy Wednesday" after the appearance of Judas in the Gospel. More importantly for us, it's the last full day of liturgical Lent, which ends tomorrow evening before the Mass of the Lord's Supper. This will give us an opportunity to hear the Third Servant Song in the light of the end of this period of purification and enlightenment, so that we can recognize with gratitude the gifts that God has given to us for the building up of the body of Christ and the mission of God's reign in the world.

The Servant celebrates a "well-trained tongue" as God's gift, to speak or sing or persuade, so that "I might...speak to the weary a word that will rouse them." What a gift to have in these days, when everyone is so weary of broken promises, false starts, joyless labor, and uninspiring religion. Like Jesus, we offer peaceful revolution of heart and spirit, one that tells the truth about the present and offers a different future in this world.

The Holy Spirit offers gifts to everyone for the good of the whole body as we work together to bring the Gospel vision to life. Thus the Servant sings, "The Lord GOD helps me," because telling the truth, especially in the face of pain, rejection, and persecution, is a fire burning within us. Life as it is, with such gross inequalities in the human family, with so many suffering at the expense of the luxury of so few, is the lie.

Lent has been a time for us to ask one another, "How is the peace of this world working out for you?" In honesty, we have to admit that things are not good, and our accommodation to and cooperation with evil has contributed to violence, poverty, and despair in the world. But that tomb can be broken open!

The one who raised Lazarus lives, he himself raised from the dead, to be resurrection and life for all. Life by life, glint by shard of divine light, the Servant of God dispels darkness even today, in this world. In the waning hours of Lent, let us pray for light to see the gifts in us that can turn the world around, that we will know the assurance of God's presence when we are called to use them.

PRACTICE: "Speak to the weary a word that will rouse them." We've listened to the Gospel this Lent. Someone you know needs to hear that there is light right in the midst of darkness. Tell them so. Be the light.

HOLY THURSDAY
EXODUS 12:1–8, 11–14; PSALMS 116:12–13, 15–16,
17–18; 1 CORINTHIANS 11:23–26; JOHN 13:1–15

In the oldest New Testament witness to the origin of the Eucharist, St. Paul in Corinthians says that the Lord's Supper proclaims the death of the Lord. Indeed, the Passover itself, in whose shadow these events occurred, is a memorial splashed with blood and death. Throughout the season of Lent, we heard over and over again the danger involved in taking up the mission of Christ. He himself describes it as "taking up the cross," and as losing one's life in order to find it.

But we know that true love, that exhilarating experience of wanting to pour ourselves out for another, is an overflow of life, and a source of deep, inexpressible joy. When the self-gift of love is complete, as it is in the *agape* of God, it might look like death, but it is never anything other than life in abundance.

Thus the great arc of the Logos in John's Gospel begins with Christ laying divinity aside to dwell among us, sees him kneeling like a slave to wash the feet of his disciples and going to the cross to die. But the Father raises him from death and glorifies him. Christ gives the Holy Spirit to the Church, sending us to continue the Father's mission upon which he himself was sent. For us, too, the mission is *agape*, the method is washing feet on the way to the cross, serving the world by pouring our lives out for others.

We have experienced the joy of love. We may not have fully learned that the love to which we are commanded includes strangers and enemies as well as family and friends.

So who is gathered at this table with us tonight? We have met them all: the revolutionary and the collaborator, Samaritan and Roman, Pharisee and tax collector, lawyer and adulteress, Lazarus and the rich man, Simon and the woman with a bad reputation, both lost sons of the parable told by one who "ate with tax collectors and sinners." The master has again "gone to eat in the house of sinners." Our house.

PRAYER: Lord Jesus, help me to do as you have done, and give my life in service to the Gospel, that all may be one. Amen.

GOOD FRIDAY
ISAIAH 52:13 — 53:12; PSALMS 31:2, 6, 12–13, 15–16, 17, 25; HEBREWS 4:14–16; 5:7–9; JOHN 18:1 — 19:42

The Fourth Song of the Suffering Servant today further expands the meaning of being God's anointed, the *Christos*, or Messiah. We hear, as it begins and ends, God speak of the Servant's exaltation, but in the heart of it, we stand and wonder with other onlookers how all this could happen, and how, through this bloody injustice, the persecution and death of an innocent person, God's will could be accomplished and the many justified.

But in Jesus, it was not simply a matter of the death of an innocent man, or even a random execution of a troublemaker by an occupying power.

Jesus is the arrival of God's empire. In his word and works, in his very person, the "kingdom of God is at hand," right before our eyes. His life outlines and exemplifies a clear alternative to the world created by other gods, and he builds a community to begin to live that alternative vision.

Jesus's enemies and antagonists don't see it. His vision sounds like blasphemy to the priests and Temple cult charged with interpreting and enforcing religious purity. It sounds like sedition to the occupying force that has its own cult, its own god, and expects cooperation if not complete obeisance from its subjects in order to preserve order.

John's Jesus, accused of setting himself up as an opponent of Caesar, tries to speak transparently: "My kingdom is not like those you know. If it were, there would be a fight. But it's not going to be like that." Hearing Jesus's claim that his life's mission is to bear witness to this truth, the confused and cynical Roman governor barks, "Truth? What does that mean?" The crowd, whoever they are, opts to free a different seditionist, a violent one. It only knows one kind of power. Sentence is pronounced, and for a few dark hours, the god of Rome wins.

The Servant's life, however, is not in Caesar's hands, but in God's. This story is not ended. As Jesus hands over his Spirit to the Father's loving care, he hands over the Spirit to those in whom his word has been planted. The grain of wheat has fallen into the earth and died. The story has just begun.

PRACTICE: Take time today to reflect on the meaning of the cross in your life.

HOLY SATURDAY / VIGIL OF EASTER
GENESIS 1:1 — 2:2 OR 1, 26–31A; GENESIS 22:1–18 OR
1–2, 9A, 10–13, 15–18; EXODUS 14:15 — 15:1; ISAIAH
54:5–14; ISAIAH 55:1–11; BARUCH 3:9–15, 32–4:4;
EZEKIEL 36:16–17A, 18–28; PSALMS 118:1–2, 16–17,
22–23; ROMANS 6:3–11

GOSPEL YEAR A: MATTHEW 28:1–10

GOSPEL YEAR B: MARK 16:1–7

GOSPEL YEAR C: LUKE 24:1–12

Finally, it comes down to this night, the story and the choice it sets before us.

Once, a people without a country were slaves to the mightiest nation of all, and they were set free and given a country and a future when one God challenged the gods of Egypt. This is the story of that God and God's people.

Once there was chaos, now there is cosmos. Once darkness, now light. Once no life, now a world, a universe, teeming with life. This is the story of the One who called light out of darkness.

Once God's people were in exile and God brought them home and called himself "Husband." Once God bound himself to a people in an unbreakable covenant, surer than the rain and snow, certain as sown seed. Once God gave a law whose words are everlasting life, a God who forgives, washes sin away, and slakes the thirst of the world that water cannot reach.

And here we come tonight, all of us slaves, in one way or another, to other gods who have claims on our lives, our time, and our resources. Here we come tonight, citizens of a dark, chaotic world within and without. Here we come tonight, certain that we are alone, unguided, unforgiven, guilty, parched, and hungry.

And once again, horse and rider are cast into the sea. Once again, God says, "Light!" and light begins to shine. Once again a voice summons all who are thirsty to come to the water.

Why? Because it was never just about what happened back then, in the remarkable time of stories. The paschal light that broke up the darkness of our Church when we entered tonight is new, light never seen before. Creation is now. Exodus is now. Resurrection is now. The newly baptized, dressed in white and redolent of scented oil, are the beaming witnesses to God's loving-kindness in the world today.

This is the night the Light broke the chains of death. *This* is the day that the Lord has made. Let us be glad and rejoice in it. Amen.

PRACTICE: Plan on sharing the joy of Easter—food, flowers, company—with someone who needs it. Someone sees just an empty tomb. Be the angel who tells them what it means.

EASTER SUNDAY
ACTS 10:34A, 37–43; PSALMS 118:1–2, 16–17, 22–23; COLOSSIANS 3:1–4 OR 1 CORINTHIANS 5:6B–8; JOHN 20:1–9

At the outset of Lent, we undertook the inner work of reflecting on the meaning of the baptismal promises to prepare for this day, so that we might be able to respond with a new integrity. Now, standing in the Easter light of the Resurrection, the victory of Jesus over the false promises of the gods of "this world," we are asked to renew those vows.

Do you renounce sin, so as to live in the freedom of the children of God? Do you renounce Satan?
"Turn away from sin, and believe the good news." We have a clear choice. The false promise of the god of death is that peace can be managed by the strong, that violence and threats can achieve an acceptable status quo for everyone. The other God is the God of life, of justice, mutual service, reconciliation, and invitation. We cannot serve both masters.

Do you believe in God, the Father almighty, Creator of heaven and earth?
To believe is to act with love. The God of Jesus, whom he told us to address as "our Father," invites us to a "kingdom" in which all have enough bread, and forgiveness is a way of life.

Do you believe in Jesus Christ, his only Son, our Lord?
The love of God was made flesh in Jesus. God is not an idea or a law. God became human like us, pouring divinity out, becoming a slave, bearing witness against the god of death. He was killed by our violent treachery. But God raised him to life again, and he lives forever.

Do you believe in the Holy Spirit, the holy Catholic Church, the communion of saints, the forgiveness of sins, the resurrection of the body, and life everlasting?
From the cross, Jesus handed over his Spirit so that Abba's mission of unity and reconciliation might go on forever in the Church.

Last night's First Reading began, "In the beginning," and ended with a command to go out and live the Gospel. We are seeds planted in God's garden, a little yeast thrown into the dough to change it and give it life. Let our "I do believe" be a new beginning, a ray of light dispelling the darkness of sin and death.

PRAYER: I do believe, Lord. Help my unbelief.

NOTES

1. *Rite of Christian Initiation of Adults*, #138. LTP © 1988, Archdiocese of Chicago

2. Quoted in David G. Creamer, *Guides for the Journey: John MacMurray, Bernard Lonergan, and James Fowler* (Washington, D.C.: University Press of America, 1996), p. 133.

3. Quoted in Ashton Applewhite, et al., eds., *And I Quote: The Definitive Collection of Quotes, Sayings, and Jokes for the Contemporary Speechmaker* (New York: Thomas Dunne, 2003), p. 106.

4. Quoted in Sallie McFague, *Life Abundant: Rethinking Theology and Economy for a Planet in Peril* (Minneapolis: Augsburg Fortress, 2000), p. 192.

5. See Stanley Hauerwas and William H. Willmon, *Resident Aliens: A Provocative Christian Assessment of Culture and Ministry for People Who Know that Something Is Wrong* (Nashville: Abingdon, 1989).

6. Quoted in Jeff Evans, *Inspirational Presence: The Art of Transformational Leadership* (Garden City, N.Y.: Morgan James, 2009), p. iv.

7. John Dominic Crossan, Jonathan L. Reed, *In Search of Paul: How Jesus' Apostle Opposed Rome's Empire with God's Kingdom* (New York: HarperCollins, 2004), p. 74.

8. Quoted in Faith S. Holsaert, ed., *Hands on the Freedom Plow: Personal Accounts by Women in SNCC* (Champaign, Ill.: University of Illinois Press, 2010), p. 219.